A BOOK OF
GRACE

Words to Bring You Peace

Edited by Margi Preus and Ann Treacy

Copyright © 2002, 2010 by Margi Preus and Ann Treacy
Cover and internal design © 2010 by Sourcebooks, Inc.
Cover design by Showcase Design
Cover image © Melanie Acevedo/Jupiter Images

Sourcebooks and the colophon are registered trademarks of Sourcebooks, Inc.

Published by Sourcebooks, Inc.
P.O. Box 4410, Naperville, Illinois 60567-4410
(630) 961-3900
Fax: (630) 961-2168
www.sourcebooks.com

Library of Congress Cataloging-in-Publication Data
Preus, Margi.
A book of grace : words to bring you peace / Margi Preus and Ann Treacy.
p. cm.
1. Prayers. I. Treacy, Ann. II. Title.
BL560 .P735 2002
291.4'33—dc21
2002001110

Printed and bound in the United States of America.
IN 10 9 8 7 6 5 4 3 2 1

May we walk with grace and may the light of the universe shine upon our path.

—Anonymous

CONTENTS

STRENGTH AND
COURAGE

O Lord, thou knowest how busy
I must be this day; if I forget thee,
do not thou forget me: for Christ's sake.

—*General Lord Astley (1579–1652)*

Commander of King Charles's forces in the
English Civil War, General Lord Astley said
this prayer before the battle of Edgehill in 1642.

Here I stand; I can do no otherwise.
God help me. Amen.

—*Martin Luther (1483–1546)*

Martin Luther led the Reformation,
the religious movement resulting
in the birth of Protestantism.

O Lord, I do not pray for tasks equal to my strength: I ask for strength equal to my tasks.

—*Phillips Brooks (1835–1893)*

Episcopal bishop of Massachusetts, author of the carol "O Little Town of Bethlehem."

May there be voice in my mouth,
breath in my nostrils,
sight in my eyes, hearing in my ears;
may my hair not turn gray
or my teeth purple;
may I have much strength in my arms.

May I have power in my thighs,
swiftness in my legs,
steadiness in my feet.
May all my limbs be uninjured and my soul
remain unconquered.

—*Hindu, Atharva-Veda XIX*

Vedas are ancient written works regarded by Hindus
as the revealed words of God. The oldest is
the Rig Veda, written before 1000 B.C.

Life has meaning only in the struggles.
Triumph or defeat is in the hands of the Gods.
So let us celebrate the struggles.

—*Swahili warrior song*

PROTECTION

Prayer of Protection

The light of God surrounds me;
The love of God enfolds me;
The power of God protects me;
The presence of God watches over me.
Wherever I am, God is.

—Anonymous

Protect us, Lord, as we stay awake;
watch over us as we sleep; that awake,
we may keep watch with Christ,
and asleep, rest in his peace.

—*Catholic antiphon at compline*

Antiphons are snippets placed at the beginning
and end of the psalm or canticle that help place it
in a liturgical context. *Compline* means night prayer.

Protect me, O Lord;
My boat is so small,
And your sea is so big.

—*Breton fisherman's prayer*

Angel sent by God to guide me,
Be my light and walk beside me.
Be my guardian and protect me,
In the paths of life direct me.

—traditional Christian prayer

Christian prayer is considered a conversation
with God. It is an important part of all
Christian worship. Some people kneel when praying,
with eyes closed and hands clasped together.

God protect this country from foe, famine, and falsehood.

*—two thousand-year-old Iranian prayer
inscribed on Shiraz airport*

WORDS FROM
THE HEART

God be in my head
And in my understanding.
God be in my eyes
And in my looking.
God be in my mouth
And in my speaking.
God be in my heart
And in my thinking.

—traditional

O God, shower us with love
For ever and ever
O God bless us
For ever and ever
O God help us
For ever and ever

—*New Zealand, Maori*

O Great Spirit, whose voice I hear in the winds
and whose breath gives life to all the world,
hear me!
I am small and weak,
I need your strength and wisdom.

Let me walk in beauty and make my eyes ever
behold the red and purple sunset.

Make my hands respect the things you have
made and my ears sharp to hear your voice.

Make me wise so that I may understand the
things you have taught my people.

Let me learn the lessons you have
hidden in every leaf and rock.

I seek strength not to be greater
than my brother, but to fight
my greatest enemy—myself.

Make me always ready to come to you with
clean hands and straight eyes.

So when life fades, as the fading sunset, my
spirit may come to you without shame.

—*Native American*

A Turu Manu

My bird, by power of charm ascending,
In the glance of an eye, like the sparrow hawk,
By this charm shall my bird arise.
My bird bestride the heavens,
Beyond the swirling waters,
Like the stars Atutahi and Rehua,
and there spread out thy wings
To the very clouds. Truly so.

For the Maori people, kites were associated with
gods and kite flying was considered a sacred ritual.
Since they believed that birds could carry messages
between themselves and the gods, the kites were
shaped like birds. Sometimes the kites represented
the gods themselves. Often the flying of a kite was
accompanied by a chant called the turu manu.

Father-Mother God,
Lovingly, Thee I seek,
Patient, meek,
In the way Thou hast,
Be it slow or fast,
Up to Thee.

—*Mary Baker Eddy (1821–1910),*
the founder of Christian Science

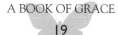

A Child's Prayer

Make me, dear Lord, polite and kind
To every one, I pray.
And may I ask you how you find
Yourself, dear Lord, today?

—*John Banister Tabb (1845–1909)*

O Jesus
Be the canoe that holds me in the sea of life.
Be the steer that keeps me straight.
Be the outrigger that supports me in times of
great temptation.
Let thy spirit be my sail that carries me
through each day.
Keep my body strong,
so that I can paddle steadfastly on,
in the long voyage of life.

—*islander's prayer from Melanesia*

I shall light a candle of understanding in thine heart, which shall not be put out.

—*the Apocrypha, Esdras, xiv, 25*

O thou great Chief, light a candle in my heart
that I may see what is therein and sweep the
rubbish from thy dwelling place.

—*African schoolgirl*

God, make my life a little light
within the world to glow;
A little flame to burn so bright,
wherever I may go.

—*England, traditional*

O heavenly Father, open wide the sluice
gate into my heart that I may receive
thy living water and be fruitful.

—*Punjabi, Christian*

The Punjab region consists of northwestern
India and a province of Pakistan.

Gracious God, oil the hinges of our hearts'
doors that they may swing gently and
easily to welcome your coming.

—*New Guinea*

Lord, make a basket of my body and a bag of my heart, and fill both full of thyself. Oh, help us serve thee!

—*Ainu woman's prayer*

O Lord
let my spirit glow so brightly,
that darkness will disappear.

—Islamic child's prayer, Pakistan

Create in me a clean heart, O God;
and renew a right spirit within me.

—Psalms 51:10, the Bible, King James Version

Grant Us Peace

Dona nobis pacem	**Latin**
Daj nam pokoj	**Polish**
Utupe sisi amani	**Swahili**
Gi oss fred	**Norwegian**
Gib uns den Frieden	**German**
Donne nous la paix	**French**
Danos la paz	**Spanish**
Tabhair dúinn síochán	**Irish Gaelic**

Deep peace of the running wave to you.
Deep peace of the flowing air to you.
Deep peace of the quiet earth to you.
Deep peace of the shining stars to you.

—*Celtic benediction*

Peace is every step.
The shining red sun is my heart.
Each flower smiles with me.
How green, how fresh all that grows.
How cool the wind blows.
Peace is every step.
It turns the endless path to joy.

—Thich Nhat Hanh (b. 1929)

Thich Nhat Hanh is a Vietnamese monk who is also
a poet, Zen master, and lifelong peace activist.
A revered Buddhist teacher, he travels the
world spreading his message of peace.

Let us know peace.
For as long as the moon shall rise,
For as long as the rivers shall flow,
For as long as the sun shall shine,
For as long as the grass shall grow,
Let us know peace.

—*Cheyenne*

O God of many names
Lover of all nations
We pray for peace
in our hearts
in our homes
in our nations
in our world
The peace of your will
The peace of our need.

—*George Appleton (1902–1993)*

Grandfather,
Look at our brokenness.
We know that in all creation
Only the human family
Has strayed from the Sacred Way.

We know that we are the ones
Who are divided.
And we are the ones
Who must come back together
To walk in the Sacred Way.

Grandfather, Sacred One,
Teach us love, compassion, and honor
That we may heal the Earth
And heal each other.

—*Ojibwe*

The Ojibwe people live in parts of the
northern United States and Canada.

I will be truthful.
I will suffer no injustice.
I will be free from fear.
I will not use force.
I will be of good will to all men.

—*Mahatma Gandhi (1869–1948)*

Gandhi was one of the greatest Indian leaders of the
1900s. He believed in nonviolent political resistance
and tolerated all religious creeds. The people of
India called him Mahatma, which means "great soul."

O God,
You are Peace.
From You comes Peace,
to You returns Peace.
Revive us with a salutation of Peace,
and lead us to Your abode of Peace.

—*Islamic*

Peaceful be Earth, peaceful heaven,
peaceful waters, peaceful trees. May
all gods bring me peace. May there be
peace through these invocations of peace.
With these invocations of peace which appease
everything, I render peaceful whatever here is
terrible, whatever here is cruel, whatever here is
sinful. Let it become auspicious, let everything
be peaceful to us.

—*Hindu, tenth century* B.C.

Prayer of St. Francis

Lord, make me an instrument of your peace.
Where there is hatred, let me sow love;
Where there is injury, pardon;
Where there is doubt, faith;
Where there is despair, hope;
Where there is darkness, light;
And where there is sadness, joy.

O, Divine Master,
Grant that I may not so much seek to be
consoled as to console;
To be understood as to understand;
To be loved as to love;
For it is in giving that we receive;
It is in pardoning that we are pardoned;
It is in dying that we are born to eternal life.
Amen.

Francis Bernardone (1181–1226) is the patron saint of
ecologists and the legendary protector of snared birds,
beaten horses, hungry dogs, and all God's creatures.

God our Father, Creator of the world,
please help us to love one another.
Make nations friendly with other nations;
make all of us love one another like brothers.
Help us to do our part to bring peace in the
world and happiness to all men.

—*Japanese*

Before me peaceful
Behind me peaceful
Under me peaceful
Over me peaceful
Around me peaceful

—Navajo

Lead me from Death to Life,
from Falsehood to Truth.
Lead me from Despair to Hope,
from Fear to Trust.
Lead me from Hate to Love,
from War to Peace.
Let Peace fill our Heart,
our World, our Universe.

—*Jain*

The Jain set aside forty-eight minutes every day to practice meditation. Many Jains have shrines in their own homes where they worship. A central belief of Jainism is respect for all living things, no matter how small. Consequently, Jains wear masks and sweep the ground in front of them to avoid causing harm to insects.

JOY

A person filled with joy preaches
without preaching.

—*Mother Teresa*

The year's at the spring
And day's at the morn;
Morning's at seven;
The hillside's dew-pearled;
The lark's on the wing;
The snail's on the thorn;
God's in His heaven—
All's right with the world!

*—from "Pippa Passes" by Robert Browning (1812–1889),
poet of Victorian England*

Now may every living thing, young or old, weak or strong, living near or far, known or unknown, living or departed or yet unborn, may every living thing be full of bliss.

—Buddha

Siddhartha Gautama became known as Buddha (or Enlightened One) beginning in northeast India around 450 B.C.

The great sea
Has set me adrift
It moves me
As the weed in a great river
Earth and the great weather
Move me
Have carried me away.
My soul is swept up in joy.

—*Uvavnuk, an Inuit shaman woman*

According to the beliefs of the Inuit, Uvavnuk received her gift of inspiration when a meteor filled her with light, transforming her into a holy person.

Good thoughts, good words, good deeds.

—the Zoroastrian ideal

During prayers (several times daily),
Zoroastrian worshippers face a source of light
and undo the kusti, a sacred cord that is
wrapped three times around the waist.

I slept and dreamt
that life was joy.
I awoke and saw
that life was service.
I served and understood that service was joy.

—*Rabindranath Tagore (1861–1941)*

Rabindranath Tagore wrote about one hundred
books of verse, fifty plays, forty works of fiction,
and fifteen books of essays. He won
the Nobel Prize for literature in 1913.

O God, I thank thee for all the joy
I have had in life.

—*Earl Brithmoth*

Grief can take care of itself, but to get the full measure of joy, you must divide it with someone.

—*Mark Twain*

O let us live in joy, in love amongst those who hate! Among those who hate, let us live in love.

O let us live in joy, in health amongst those who are ill! Among those who are ill, let us live in health.

O let us live in joy, although having nothing! In joy let us live like spirits of light.

—*from the Dhammapada (India), a collection of 423 Buddhist teachings dating from the sixth century* B.C.

THANKSGIVING

Thank God for rain
and the beautiful rainbow colors,
and thank God for letting children
splash in the puddles.

—*English child's prayer*

If our mouths were as full of song as
the sea and our tongues as full of
melody as the endless waves, and our
lips as full of praise as the heavens,
and our eyes as bright as the sun and moon, and
our hands outstretched like eagle's
wings and our feet as swift as a gazelle's,
we still could not thank You enough for the
thousands upon thousands of favors You have
bestowed upon us and our ancestors.

—*Jewish*

Father, We Thank Thee

For flowers that bloom about our feet,
Father, we thank Thee,
For tender grass so fresh and sweet,
Father, we thank Thee,
For the song of bird and hum of bee,
For all things fair we hear or see,
Father in heaven, we thank Thee.

For blue of stream and blue of sky,
Father, we thank Thee,
For pleasant shade of branches high,
Father, we thank Thee,
For fragrant air and cooling breeze,
For beauty of the blooming trees,
Father in heaven, we thank Thee.

For this new morning with its light,
Father, we thank Thee,
For rest and shelter of the night,
Father we thank Thee,
For health and food, for love and friends,
For everything Thy goodness sends,
Father in heaven, we thank Thee.

—*Ralph Waldo Emerson (1803–1882)*

Ralph Waldo Emerson was an American poet
and essayist of the Transcendental movement,
a nineteenth-century movement of New England
writers who believed that all of creation shares
unity and that all people are basically good.

Praised be you, my Lord,
with all your creatures,
especially Brother Sun,
who gives light to the day and enlightens us
by your will,
radiant, beautiful, and eminently splendid,
he is an image of you, Lord of all.

Praised be you, my Lord,
through Sister Moon
and the Stars
shining brightly,
stunning in appearance.

Praise and bless my Lord and
give him thanks
and serve him with great humility.

—adapted from "Canticle of Brother Sun"
by Saint Francis

All the cattle are resting in the fields,
The trees and plants are growing,
The birds flutter above the marshes,
Their wings uplifted in adoration,
And all the sheep are dancing,
All winged things are flying,
They live when you have shone on them.

—*ancient Egyptian*

O Lord, that lends me life,
Lend me a heart replete with thankfulness.

—*from* King Henry VI, Part II *by*
William Shakespeare (1564–1616)

GRACE BEFORE
MEALS

This ritual is one.
The food is one.
We who offer the food are one.
The fire of hunger is also one.
All action is one.
We who understand this are one.

—*ancient Hindu*

The bread is pure and fresh,
the water is cool and clear.
Lord of all life, be with us,
Lord of all life, be near.

—*African*

Bless us, O Lord,
And these, Thy gifts,
Which we are about to receive
From Thy bounty
Through Christ, our Lord.
Amen.

—traditional

Thank you for the wind and rain
and sun and pleasant weather.
Thank you for this our food
and that we are together.

—*Mennonite*

This food comes from the earth and the sky,
It is the gift of the entire universe
And the fruit of much hard work;
I vow to live a life which is worthy to receive it.

—*Buddhist*

Buddhists pray in an attempt to combine
their inner thoughts with good forces, rather
than as a way of asking for something.

Make us worthy, Lord, to serve our fellow men throughout the world who live and die in poverty or hunger. Give them, through our hands this day, their daily bread, and by our understanding love, give peace and joy.

—*Mother Teresa of Calcutta (1910–1997)*

Mother Teresa founded the Missionaries of Charity. For her humanitarian work with "the poorest of the poor," she won the Nobel Peace Prize in 1979.

Graces by Robert Burns

(Before the meal)
O Thou who kindly dost provide
for every creature's want!
We bless Thee, God of Nature wide,
For all thy goodness lent.
And, if it please Thee, heavenly guide,
may never worse be sent;
but, whether granted or denied,
Lord bless us with content.

—*Robert Burns*

(After the meal)
O Thou, in whom we live and move,
Who made the sea and shore;
Thy goodness constantly we prove,
and grateful would adore;
and, if it please Thee, Power above.
Still grant us with such store
the friend we trust, the fair we love,
And we desire no more.

—*Robert Burns*

Robert Burns (1759–1796), was a
Scottish farmer, poet, and songwriter.

Bread

Be gentle when you touch Bread.
Let it not lie
Uncared for,
Unwanted.
So often Bread
Is taken for granted.

Beauty of patient toil.
Wind and rain
Have caressed it.
Christ often blessed it.
Be gentle when you touch Bread.

—*Anonymous*

Mother Earth, you who give us food, whose children we are and on whom we depend, please make this produce you give us flourish and make our children and animals grow… Children, the Earth is the mother of man because she gives him food.

—*Rigoberta Menchú*

Rigoberta Menchú is the 1992 Nobel Peace Prize winner. She is a Mayan-Quiche woman from Guatemala who became a voice for the indigenous peoples of her country.

O God,
bless this food we are about to receive.
Give bread to those who hunger,
and give hunger for justice
to those who have bread.

—*Nicaraguan*

Now that I am about to eat, O Great Spirit,
give my thanks to the beasts and birds whom
You have provided for my hunger; and pray
deliver my sorrow that living things must make
a sacrifice for my comfort and well-being.
Let the feather of corn spring up in its time and
let it not wither but make full grains
for the fires of our cooking pots,
now that I am about to eat.

—*Native American*

Let those who have need of more
ask for it humbly.
And let those who have need of less
thank God.

—*the Rule of St. Benedict*

Be present at our table, Lord;
Be here and everywhere adored.
These mercies bless, and grant that we
May feast in paradise with thee.
Amen.

—*attributed to John Cennick (1718–1755)*

Praised are You, Adonai our God, Guide of the Universe, who creates innumerable living beings and their needs, for all the things You have created to sustain every living being. Praised are You, the Life of the Universe.

—Jewish blessing

The Star of David is a symbol of the Jewish faith meant to represent the shield or emblem of King David. The two entwined triangles are symbols of good luck. One triangle faces heavenward, while the opposing one faces Earth. This symbol appears on the flag of the state of Israel and is known as the Magen David (shield of David).

Let us live together, eat together.
Together, let us do noble deeds
and share the fruits.
Let us understand each other,
casting aside jealousy and ill-will.
Let us all work for peace and peace alone.

—Hindu

For Hindus, the simplest and most important prayer,
or mantra, is the saying of the sacred word Om to
make contact with the divine. Om or Aum is the
eternal syllable. It is believed to contain the secrets
of the universe; it is said or sung before and
after all prayers.

A circle of friends is a blessed thing.
Sweet is the breaking of bread with friends.
For the honor of their presence at our board
We are deeply grateful, Lord.

Thanks be to Thee for friendship shared,
Thanks be to Thee for food prepared.
Bless Thou the cup; bless Thou the bread;
Thy blessing rest upon each head.

—*Walter Rauschenbusch*

Mother, Father, God,
For the sacred circle of family and friendship,
we thank you and ask that, with your
guidance, we may widen and deepen those
circles by touching others with love and
understanding. Blessings be.

—*Sue Patton Thoele*

We cannot love God unless we love each other,
and to love we must know each other.
We know him in the breaking of bread,
and we are not alone any more.
Heaven is a banquet and life is a banquet, too,
even with a crust, where
there is companionship.
Love comes with community.

—*Dorothy Day (1897–1980)*

Dorothy Day was an American journalist who pro-
moted social change and defended workers.
She established many hospitality houses for
the homeless during the Great Depression
of the 1930s. Soup kitchens are often
called Dorothy Day Centers in her memory.

SERENITY AND
COMFORT

I don't think of all the misery,
but of all the beauty that still remains.

—*Anne Frank*

God, give us grace to accept with serenity
the things that cannot be changed,
courage to change the things that
should be changed, and the wisdom to
distinguish one from the other.

—Reinhold Niebuhr (1892–1971),
American Protestant theologian

Hold on to what is good even
if it is a handful of earth.
Hold on to what you believe even
if it is a tree which stands by itself.
Hold on to what you must do even
if it is a long way from here.
Hold on to life even when it is easier letting go.
Hold on to my hand even when
I have gone away from you.

—*Pueblo*

However long the night, the dawn will break.

—*Hausa proverb (Africa)*

Slow Me Down, Lord

Ease the pounding of my heart by
the quieting of my mind.
Steady my hurried pace with a vision
of the eternal reach of time.
Give me, amid the confusion of the day,
the calmness of the everlasting hills.

Break the tensions of my nerves and muscles
with the soothing music of the singing
streams that live in my memory,
that help me to know the magical
restoring power of sleep.

Teach me the art of taking minute vacations—
of slowing down to look at a flower,
to chat with a friend,
to pat a dog, to read a few lines from a good book.

Remind me each day of the fable
of the hare and the tortoise,
that I may know that the race is
not always to the swift—
that there is more to life than increasing speed.

Let me look upward into the
branches of the towering oak
and know that it grew great and strong
because it grew slowly and well.

Slow me down, Lord, and
inspire me to send my roots
deep into the soil of life's enduring values
that I may grow toward the
stars of my greater destiny.

—*Richard Cardinal Cushing (1895–1970)*

O God
help me
to believe
the truth about myself
no matter
how beautiful it is!

—*Macrina Wiederkehr, a Benedictine sister and author*

DISAPPOINTMENT

Prayer of an Unknown Confederate Soldier

I asked for strength that I might achieve;
I was made weak that I might
learn humbly to obey.

I asked for health that I might do greater things;
I was given infirmity that
I might do better things.

I asked for riches that I might be happy;
I was given poverty that I might be wise.

I asked for power that
I might have the praise of men;
I was given weakness that
I might feel the need of God.

I asked for all things that I might enjoy life;
I was given life that I might enjoy all things.

I got nothing that I had asked for,
but everything that I had hoped for.

Almost despite myself my unspoken prayers
were answered;
I am, among all men, most richly blessed.

Troubles are often the means
God uses to fashion people into
something better than they are.

—*Anonymous*

FORGIVENESS

If anyone has hurt me or harmed me, knowingly
or unknowingly, in thought, word, or deed,
I freely forgive them.
And I, too, ask forgiveness if I have hurt anyone
or harmed anyone, knowingly or
unknowingly, in thought, word, or deed.

May I be happy
May I be peaceful
May I be free

May my friends be happy
May my friends be peaceful
May my friends be free

May my enemies be happy
May my enemies be peaceful
May my enemies be free

May all things be happy
May all things be peaceful
May all things be free.

—*Buddhist*

In the Tibetan mountains, Buddhists use prayer
wheels which contain hundreds of prayers.
When the wheels are set to spinning,
temple-goers believe the prayers fly to
all corners of the world.

Forgiveness is the fragrance the
violet sheds on the heel that crushed it.

—*Mark Twain*

All that we ought to have thought,
and have not thought,
All that we ought to have said,
and have not said,
All that we ought to have done,
and have not done;

All that we ought not to have thought,
and yet have thought,
All that we ought not to have spoken,
and yet have spoken,
all that we ought not to have done,
and yet have done;
For thoughts, words, and works, pray we,
O God, for forgiveness.

—*from an ancient Persian prayer*

PATIENCE AND
TOLERANCE

Lord, give me patience in tribulation and
grace in everything to conform my will to yours,
that I may truly say: "Your will be done,
on Earth as it is in heaven." The things,
good Lord, that I pray for, give me
your grace to labor for.

—*Sir Thomas More (1477–1535)*

O Lord, help me not to despise or
oppose what I do not understand.

*—William Penn (1644–1718) founded Pennsylvania
as a haven for persecuted Quakers and an
experiment in religious community.*

He that is slow to anger is better
than the mighty;
And he that rules his spirit better
than he that takes a city.

—*Proverbs 16:32, the Bible,*
New American Standard Version

PURITY AND
SIMPLICITY

O our Father the Sky,
hear us and make us bold.
O our Mother the Earth,
hear us and give us support.
O Spirit of the East,
send us your wisdom.
O Spirit of the South,
may we walk your path of life.
O Spirit of the West,
may we always be ready for the long journey.
O Spirit of the North,
purify us with your cleansing winds.

—Sioux

Many Native Americans consider the natural
world to be the dwelling place of the Great Spirit.
The Sioux know this spirit as Wakan Tanka.

Let nothing disturb you,
Let nothing frighten you;
Everything passes away
Except God;
And God alone suffices.

—*St. Teresa of Avila (1515–1582)*

Saint Teresa founded sixteen convents
of a new order, known as the "barefoot"
Carmelites because of their simple lifestyle.

Grant me the ability to be alone;
may it be my custom to go outdoors each day
among the trees and grasses,
among all growing things,
and there may I be alone,
to talk with the One
that I belong to.

—*Rabbi Nachman of Bratslav (1771–1811),*
Polish Hasidic teacher and storyteller

GENEROSITY

Lord, teach me to be generous
Teach me to serve you as you deserve.
To give and not to count the cost;
To fight and not to heed the wounds;
To toil and not to seek for rest;
To labor and not to ask for reward,
Except to know that I am doing your will.
Amen.

—*attributed to St. Ignatius of Loyola (1491–1556)*

Amen is a Semitic root connected with faith and believing. *Amen* means, "I believe this," or "this is trustworthy." Christians took the Hebrew word over into Greek and thus it became a part of Christian prayer.

Do all the good you can,
In all the ways you can,
In all the places you can,
At all times you can,
To all people you can,
As long as ever you can.

—*John Wesley (1703–1792)*

LOVE

What is love? To rank the effort above the prize may be called love.

—*Confucius, c. 500* B.C.

Love consists in sharing
what one has
and what one is
with those one loves.

Love ought to show itself in deeds
more than in words.

*—St. Ignatius of Loyola (1491–1556),
the Spanish nobleman who founded the Jesuits*

The best and most beautiful things
in the world cannot be seen
or even touched. They must be felt with the
heart.

—*Helen Keller*

Someday, after we have mastered the winds,
the wave, the tides, and gravity, we shall
harness for God the energies of love. Then,
for the second time in the history of the world,
man will have discovered fire.

—*Teilhard de Chardin (1881–1955)*

Love all God's creation, the whole and every grain of sand in it. Love every leaf, every ray of God's light. Love the animals, love the plants, love everything. If you love everything, you will perceive the divine mystery in things. Once you perceive it, you will begin to comprehend it better every day. And you will come at last to love the whole world with an all-embracing love.

—*from* The Brothers Karamozov *by Fyodor Dostoyevsky (1821–1881)*

FAMILY

Dear God, our Father,
thank you for caring for each of us:
for our mothers and fathers,
for sisters and brothers,
for food each day,
for time to play,
for pets to love,
for the sky above.
Amen.

—*Debbie Trafton O'Neal*

May there always be sunshine
May there always be blue skies
May there always be Mama
May there always be me.

—*Russian folk song*

To thee, the Creator, to thee, the Powerful,
I offer this fresh bud,
New fruit of the ancient tree.
Thou art the master, we thy children.
To thee, the Creator, to thee, the Powerful,
Kmvoum,[1] Kmvoum,
I offer this new plant.

—*Pygmies, Zaire*

1. God

YOUTH, AGE, AND GENDER

Pretty much all the honest truth-telling
there is in the world is done by children.

—*Oliver Wendell Holmes*

What is learned in the cradle lasts 'til the grave.

—Hungarian

She openeth her mouth with wisdom;
and in her tongue is the law of kindness.

—*Proverbs 31:26, the Bible, King James Version*

I am the woman who holds up the sky.
The rainbow runs through my eyes.
The sun makes a path to my womb.
My thoughts are in the shape of clouds.
But my words are yet to come.

—*Ute*

FRIENDS

There is no one-way friendship.

—*Masai*

O Lord, give me strength that the whole world look to me with the eyes of a friend. Let us ever examine each other with the eyes of a friend.

—*Hindu Veda*

Oh, the comfort, the inexpressible comfort
of feeling safe with a person, having neither
to weigh thought nor measure words, but
pouring them all right out, just as they are,
chaff and grain together, certain that a
faithful hand will take and sift them, keep
what is worth keeping, and with a breath of
kindness, blow the rest away.

—*Shoshone*

ANIMALS AND
NATURE

Hurt No Living Thing

Hurt no living thing;
Ladybird, nor butterfly,
Nor moth with dusty wing,
Nor cricket chirping cheerily,
Nor grasshopper so light of leap,
Nor dancing gnat, nor beetle fat,
Nor harmless worms that creep.

—*Christina Rossetti*

The dog was created specially for children. He is the god of frolic.

—*Henry Ward Beecher*

Loving Mother,
hear and bless
thy beasts
and singing birds.
And guard with tenderness
small things
that have no words.

—*traditional Christian prayer, adapted*

That each day I may walk unceasingly
on the banks of my water, that my soul
may repose on the branches of the trees which
I planted, that I may refresh myself under the
shadow of my sycamore.

—inscription on Egyptian tomb, c. 1400 B.C.

Sycamore trees were considered sacred in ancient
Egypt. The goddess Hathor was supposed to have
lived in the branches of a sycamore from where she
dispensed sustenance and water to deceased souls.

The Creation

All things bright and beautiful,
All creatures great and small,
All things wise and wonderful,
The Lord God made them all.

Each little flower that opens,
Each little bird that sings,
He made their glowing colors,
He made their tiny wings.

The tall trees in the greenwood,
The meadows where we play,
The rushes by the water
We gather every day—

He gave us eyes to see them,
And lips that we might tell
How great is God Almighty,
Who has made all things well!

—*Cecil Frances Alexander*

The Grasshopper's Song—from Israel

A scraping sound: The grasshopper
In the field does purr and whir-r-r.

"Come forth, grasshoppers, come to dance,
And chant to God your lovely chants.

"Let all who can, be heard and seen
With pirouette and tambourine.

"For none shall hide where grass is deep,
But if you've legs, arise and leap!

"All that are here, respond, proclaim:
Blessed is He and blessed His name!

"Blessed be God who for our sake
This happy summertime did make.

"A plenteous feast in field and fen,
Enough for all.—Amen, amen!"

—H. N. Bialik, *translated by Jessie Sampter*

When My Dog Died

When my dog died,
I didn't cry.
I didn't even speak—
not one word.
Then I found his collar
in the closet.
It was made of thick, red leather
with a brass buckle.
I held it in my hands
and then I cried
and made his collar wet.

—*Freya Littledale*

The Prayer of the Goldfish

O God,
forever I turn in this hard crystal,
so transparent, yet I can find no way out.
Lord,
deliver me from the cramp of this water
and these terrifying things I see through it.
Put me back in the play of Your torrents,
in Your limpid springs.
let me no longer be a little goldfish
in its prison of glass,
but a living spark
in the gentleness of Your reeds.
Amen.

—*Carmen Bernos de Gasztold*

All you big things, bless the Lord
Mount Kilimanjaro and Lake Victoria
The Rift Valley and the Serengeti Plain
Fat baobabs and shady mango trees
All eucalyptus and tamarind trees
Bless the Lord
Praise and extol Him for ever and ever.

All you tiny things, bless the Lord
Busy black ants and hopping fleas
Wriggling tadpoles and mosquito larvae
Flying locusts and water drops
Pollen dust and tsetse flies
Millet seeds and dried dagaa
Bless the Lord
Praise and extol him for ever and ever.

—*African canticle*

INSPIRATION

Be like the bird, who
Halting in his flight
On limb too slight
Feels it give way beneath him,
Yet sings
Knowing he hath wings.

—*Victor Hugo*

A Song of Greatness

When I hear the old men
Telling of heroes,
Telling of great deeds
Of ancient days,
When I hear them telling,
Then I think within me
I, too, am one of these.

When I hear the people
Praising great ones,
Then I know that I, too,
Shall be esteemed,
I, too, when my time comes
Shall do mightily.

—*Ojibwe song, transcribed by Mary Austin*

Lord of the Mountain,
Reared within the Mountain
Young Man, Chieftain,
Here's a young man's prayer!
Hear a prayer for cleanness.
Keeper of the strong rain,
Drumming on the mountain;
Lord of the small rain
That restores the earth in newness;
Keeper of the clean rain,
Hear a prayer for wholeness,
Young Man, Chieftain,
Hear a prayer for fleetness,
Keeper of the deer's way,

Reared among the eagles,
Clear my feet of slothfulness
Hear a prayer for courage.
Lord of the thin peaks,
Reared amid the thunder;
Keeper of the headlands
Holding up the harvest,
Keeper of the strong rocks
Hear a prayer for staunchness.
Young Man, Chieftain,
Spirit of the Mountain.

—*Navajo*

Use what talents you possess: the woods would be very silent if no birds sang there except those that sang best.

—*Henry Van Dyke*

Our hearts are like a book full of mistakes.
Take thy eraser, Lord, and erase all our faults.

—prayer of a Christian boy from Cameroon

I believe in the sun even when it is not shining.
I believe in love even when feeling it not.
I believe in God even when he is silent.

—*inscription on the walls of a cellar in Cologne, Germany,
where Jews hid from the Nazis*

WORK

May there always be work for your hands to do
May your purse always hold a coin or two
May the sun always shine upon your
window pane
May a rainbow be certain to follow each rain
May the hand of a friend always
be near you and
May God fill your heart with gladness
to cheer you.

—*traditional Irish blessing*

Blessed is he who has found his work.

—Thomas Carlyle

O Lord God, who has called us your servants to ventures of which we cannot see the ending, by paths as yet untrodden and through perils unknown, give us faith to go out with good courage, not knowing where we go, but only that your hand is leading us and your love supporting us. Amen.

—*prayer of parting at Holden Village*

SPECIAL DAYS

Monday's child is fair of face.
Tuesday's child is full of grace.
Wednesday's child is full of woe.
Thursday's child has far to go.
Friday's child is loving and giving.
Saturday's child has to work for its living.
But the child that is born on the Sabbath Day
is fair and wise and good and gay.

—*unknown*

God bless all the aunties,
Who are kind to girls and boys;
God bless all the uncles
Who remember birthday toys.

—*a child's prayer*

My father, all last year you took care of me and now you have given me a birthday. I thank you for all your goodness and kindness to me. You have given me loving parents, a home, gifts and clothes. Thank you, God. Help me to be a better child in my new year, to grow strong, to study well, to work happily.

—*India*

BEDTIME

Good night! Good night!
Far flies the light;
But still God's love
Shall flame above,
Making all bright.
Good night! Good night!

—*Victor Hugo*

May our sleep be deep and soft,
So our work be fresh and hard.

—from St. Patrick's evening prayer

Born in the fourth century, St. Patrick is known as
the patron saint of Ireland. Tradition states that as he
traveled the green countryside, he often used
the shamrock as a symbol to explain the three
beings of the trinity—the Father, Son, and Holy Spirit.

Sleep, my babe, and peace attend thee,
All through the night;
Guardian angels, God will lend thee,
All through the night;
Soft the drowsy hours are creeping,
Hill and vale in slumber sleeping,
Mother dear her watch is keeping,
All through the night.

—*Welsh hymn*

When my sun of life is low,
When the dewy shadows creep,
Say for me before I go,
"Now I lay me down to sleep."

—*Bert Leston Taylor (1866–1921)*

A BOOK OF GRACE

Lord, of thee three things I pray:
to see thee more clearly,
love thee more dearly,
follow thee more nearly,
day by day.

—*Richard of Chichester (1197–1253)*

Richard de Wych was so poor as a student at Oxford
that he had to share a college gown with two friends,
thus having to take turns attending lectures. He grew
up to become the bishop of Chichester.

MORNING

Every day is a messenger of God.

—*Russian*

Earth, our mother,
breathe and awaken,
leaves are stirring,
all things moving,
new day coming,
life renewing.

—*Pawnee*

Blessed are you, O Lord, our God,
Ruler of the universe,
Who removes sleep from my eyes,
And slumber from my eyelids.

—*Jewish*

Now, before I run to play,
Let me not forget to pray
to God who kept me through the night
And waked me with the morning light.

Help me, Lord, to love you more
Than I ever loved before,
In my work and in my play
Please be with me through the day.

—*unknown*

Morning Prayer of St. Patrick

I arise today
through the strength of heaven,
light of the sun,
radiance of the moon,
splendor of fire,
speed of lightning,
swiftness of the wind,
depth of the sea,
stability of the earth,
firmness of the rock.

I arise today
through God's strength to pilot me,
God's might to uphold me,
God's wisdom to guide me,
God's eye to look before me,

God's ear to hear me,
God's word to speak for me,
God's hand to guard me,
God's way to lie before me,
God's shield to protect me,
God's hosts to save me
from the snares of the devil,
from everyone who desires me ill,
afar and near,
alone or in a multitude.

—*ancient Celtic prayer*

This prayer is often called "St. Patrick's Breastplate" because it was thought to protect him from hostile powers. It is also known as "The Song of the Deer" or "The Deer's Cry," a reference to the legend that God once transformed Patrick and his companions into a herd of deer to save them from their enemies.

Waking up this morning, I smile.
Twenty-four brand new hours are before me.
I vow to live fully in each moment
and to look at all beings with
eyes of compassion.

—*Thich Nhat Hanh*

With the first light of sun—
Bless you
When the long day is done—
Bless you
In your smiles and your tears—
Bless you
Through each day of your years—
Bless you

—*Irish blessing*

Look to this day,
For it is life,
For yesterday is but a dream,
And tomorrow is only a vision,
But today, well lived,
Makes every yesterday a dream of happiness
And every tomorrow a vision of hope.

—*Sanskrit proverb*

Morning has broken
Like the first morning
Blackbird has spoken
Like the first bird.
Praise for the singing!
Praise for the morning!
Praise for them, springing
Fresh from the Word!

—*from* The Children's Bells
by Eleanor Farjeon (1881–1965)

When the day returns, call us up with morning faces and with morning hearts, eager to labor, happy if happiness be our portion, and if the day be marked
for sorrow, strong to endure.

—*Robert Louis Stevenson*

Robert Louis Stevenson was a Scottish poet and writer of such classics as *Treasure Island* and *Kidnapped.* He wrote this prayer the day before he died of a stroke at age forty-four.

BLESSINGS FOR
THE HOME

Prayer for This House

May nothing evil cross this door,
And may ill-fortune never pry
About these windows; may the roar
And rains go by.

Strengthened by faith, the rafters will
Withstand the battering of the storm.
This hearth, though all the world grow chill
Will keep you warm.

Peace shall walk softly through these rooms,
Touching your lips with holy wine,
'Til every casual corner blooms
Into a shrine.

Laughter shall drown the raucous shout
And, though the sheltering walls are thin,
May they be strong to keep hate out
And hold love in.

—*Louis Untermeyer*

May the person who is going to live in this
house have many children; may he be
rich; may he be honest to people and good to
the poor; may he not suffer from
disease or any other kind of trouble;
may he be safe all these years.

—*Nyola, Kenya*

A Prayer for a Little Home

God send us a little home,
To come back to, when we roam.

Low walls, and fluted tiles,
Wide windows, a view for miles.

Red firelight and deep chairs,
Small white beds upstairs—

Great talk in little nooks,
Dim colors, rows of books.

One picture on each wall,
Not many things at all.

God send us a little ground.
Tall trees standing round.

Homely flowers in brown sod.
Overhead, thy stars, O God!

God bless, when winds blow,
Our home, and all we know.

—*Florence Bone*

Peace be to this house
And to all who dwell in it.
Peace be to them that enter
And to them that depart.

—unknown

BLESSINGS

May the blessing of God rest upon you,
May his peace abide with you,
May his presence illuminate your heart
Now and forevermore.

—*Sufi blessing*

Sufis use song, dance, and drumming to focus all their attention on Allah. A brotherhood of Sufis became known as "whirling dervishes" for their energetic dancing style that they hope will ultimately bring them into direct experience of Allah.

May Shamash[1] give you your heart's desire
May he let you see with your eyes the thing
accomplished which your lips have spoken;
May he open a path for you where it is blocked,
and a road for your feet to tread.
May he open the mountains for your crossing,
and may the nighttime bring you the
blessings of night, and Lugulbanada, your
guardian god, stand beside you for
victory.
May you have victory in the battle as though
you fought with a child.

—*ancient Babylonian*

1. the sun god

O our Mother the Earth, O our Father the sky,
Your children are we, and with tired backs
We bring you gifts that you love.
Then weave for us a garment of brightness;
May the warp be the white light of morning,
May the weft be the red light of evening,
May the fringes be the falling rain,
May the border be the standing rainbow.
Thus weave for us a garment of brightness,
That we may walk fittingly where birds sing,
That we may walk fittingly where grass is green,
O our Mother the Earth, O our Father the sky!

—*Tewa Pueblo*

Earth, arise in each of us.

—*Anonymous*

Poems by Hannah Szenes

My God, my God, I pray that these things
never end.
The sand and the sea, the rush of the waters,
The crash of the heavens, the prayer
of the heart.
The sand and the sea, the rush of the waters,
The crash of the heavens, the prayer
of the heart.

—*Hannah Szenes (1921–1944)*

Blessed is the match that burned
and kindled flames,
Blessed is the flame that set hearts on fire.
Blessed are the hearts that knew
how to die with honor.
Blessed is the match that burned,
and kindled flames.

—Hannah Szenes

Hannah Szenes was born in Budapest, Hungary. In 1943, she was one of thirty-three people chosen to parachute behind enemy lines in an attempt to warn Jewish communities in Yugoslavia about the Nazis. She was captured and tortured, but refused to divulge any information. These two poems were written shortly before her death by firing squad.

May the blessing of light be with you—
light outside and light within.
May sunlight shine upon you and warm your
heart 'til it glows like a great peat fire so that
the stranger may come and be warmed by it,
and also a friend.
May a blessed light shine out of the two eyes of
you like a candle set in two windows of a
house, bidding the wanderer to come in out
of the storm.
May the blessing of rain—the sweet, soft rain—
fall upon your spirit and wash it fair and clean.
May it leave many a shining pool where the
blue of heaven shines, and sometimes a star.
May the blessing of earth—the good,
rich earth—be with you.

May you ever have a kindly greeting for those
you pass as you go along its roads.
May the earth rest easy over you when at the
last you lie under it.
May the earth rest so lightly over you that your
spirit may be out from under it quickly, and up,
and off, and on its way to God.

—*traditional Irish blessing*

Litany of Contradictory Things

Wheat and weeds:
let them grow together.
Rich and poor:
let them grow together.
Winter, spring, summer, fall:
let them grow together.
All the seasons of one's life:
let them grow together.
Joys and sorrow, laughter, tears:
let them grow together.
Strength and weakness:
let them grow together.

Doubt and faith:
let them grow together.
Contemplation and action:
let them grow together.
Giving and receiving:
let them grow together.
The helpful and the helpless:
let them grow together.
Wisdom of the East and West:
let them grow together.
All contrarieties of the Lord:
let them grow together.

—Michael Moynahan, *Society of Jesus, adapted*

Aaronic Blessing

The Lord bless you and keep you;
The Lord make his face to shine upon you,
and be gracious unto you:
The Lord lift up his countenance upon you,
And give you peace.

—Numbers 6:24-26, the Bible,
Revised Standard Version

ACKNOWLEDGMENTS

Grateful acknowledgement is made to those who have given us permission to use their copyrighted material. Every effort has been made to trace and contact original sources. If you have not received our correspondence, please contact us for inclusion in future editions.

Pg. 34 "Peace is every step" Reprinted from *The Long Road Turns to Joy: a Guide to Walking Meditation* (1996) by Thich Nhat Hanh with permission of Parallax Press, Berkeley, California.

Pg. 36 "O God of many names" Reprinted from *The Oxford Book of Prayer,* ed. by George Appleton(1985) with permission of the Oxford University Press, Oxford, England.

Pg. 88 "Slow Me Down, Lord" by Richard Cardinal Cushing. Reprinted with permission of the Archbishop's Office, Boston, MA.

Pg. 90 "O God help me. . ." from *Seasons of Your Heart: Prayers and Reflections* by Macrina Wiederkehr, copyright © 1991 by Macrina Wiederkehr. Reprinted by permission of HarperCollins Publishers, Inc.

Pg. 108 "Grant me the ability" attributed to Nahman of Bratslav (Hasidic Rabbi) by his disciple Nathan Sternhartz of Nemirov in *Likutey Tefilah*, part two, 11; translated by Shamai Kanter (from *Kol Haneshemah*, the Reconstructionist Press, Wyncote, PA, 1996).

Pg. 110 "Lord, teach me to be generous" Adapted or reprinted from *Hearts on Fire: Praying with Jesuits*, copyright © 1993 (with permission from the Institute of Jesuit Sources, Saint Louis, MO).

Pg. 115 "Love consists in sharing" Adapted or reprinted from *Hearts on Fire: Praying with Jesuits*, copyright © 1993 (with permission from the Institute of Jesuit Sources, Saint Louis, MO).

Pg. 120 "Dear God, our Father" Reprinted by permission from *Thank You For This Food* by Debbie Trafton O'Neal, copyright ©1994 Augsburg Fortress.

Pg. 139 "The Grasshopper's Song" by H. N. Bialik. Reprinted by permission of the Union of American Hebrew Congregations Press, N.Y., N.Y.

ABOUT THE AUTHORS

Margi Preus is a playwright, director, educator, and children's book author. Visit her at www.margipreus.com.

As a registered dietitian, **Ann Treacy's** interest in nutrition has expanded to include nourishment for the soul. She enjoys writing on a variety of topics and has published various religious articles as well as fiction.